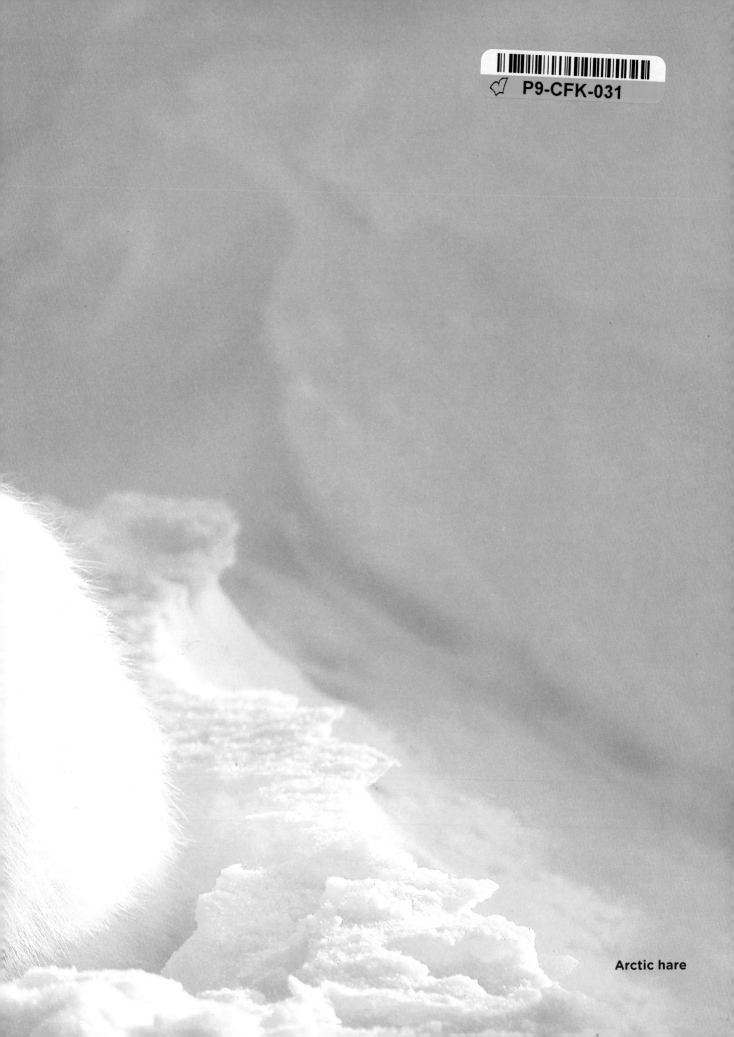

Arctic hare

Weddell seal

ANIMAL
BITES

polar
animals

Laaren Brown

how to use this book

Look for these colorful tabs to guide your Animal Bites adventure.

where they live Explore different animal habitats and ecosystems

polar bear When you see a tab this color, get a close-up look at amazing animals

how they live Learn how animals behave and adapt to their environment

vista See awesome photos that show the places animals live

big data Find the facts and figures

animal gallery Take a look at animal similarities and differences

living/working **conservation** Find out different ways people interact with animals and their habitats

Just like me
Look for this feature to see how animals behave and live like humans.

table of contents

Life in a cold climate

Snow...wind...freezing cold. How do animals survive the Arctic winter?

Polar bear

Sure, polar bears have warm fur coats. But what really helps keep them going is a thick layer of fat under the skin. A plump polar bear might have more than 4 inches of fat!

Bundle up!

How do you keep warm outside in the winter? A down coat keeps body warmth from escaping.

Arctic fox

The arctic fox's fur has a soft, thick underlayer that holds warm air near the body.

Musk ox

Musk oxen have long, dark hair that hangs down almost to the ground. Each hair is hollow, and each little space in each hair is full of air. This helps them stay warm.

Why live there?

Polar animals are perfectly adapted to cold climates. The weather doesn't bother them, and they face far fewer predators than they would in other places.

Slow food

This small sea snail feeds on algae and lichen on Alaska's rocky shorelines. It moves *slooowly*, only about 3 feet a month.

Fresh, not frozen

Many fish would freeze in icy polar waters, but the cold waters are home to many animals, such as the arctic cod, Greenland shark, squid, shrimp, and jellies, that can survive in cold water.

Berry good!

Lemmings snack on grasses, sedges, moss, and berries. But they have to be careful. All meat-eating birds and mammals in the Arctic hunt lemmings year round; they are the main meal for arctic foxes and snowy owls.

Salad bar

Plant-eating mammals like the reindeer eat greens for every meal. The tundra is home to more than 1,700 types of plant, moss, and lichen.

The big sleep

The arctic ground squirrel is the only Arctic animal that hibernates—it feasts on plants and seeds before settling into its den to sleep through the winter. This helps it save energy and survive the coldest months.

What's up, what's down?

The North Pole is up. It's a point underwater in the middle of the Arctic Circle. The South Pole is down, on the continent of Antarctica. Both areas are huge—about 5.5 million square miles.

Who lives there?

About 2 million people live in the Arctic Circle, mostly native peoples who live in the countries at its edge. There's no permanent population on Antarctica. Between 1,000 (winter) and 5,000 (summer) people live at research centers.

Arctic Circle

Antarctic Circle

Fuel turns to slush and planes can't fly in the cold South Pole winter, making it unreachable for much of the year.

That's extreme!

Summer up north means it's winter down south, and vice versa.

North Pole

| Summer | 32° |
| Winter | --40° |

South Pole

| Summer | --10° |
| Winter | --76° |

DEGREES FAHRENHEIT! ↑

Arctic Circle

Many land and ocean mammals, birds, and other creatures make their homes within the Arctic Circle. Food is scarce in winter, but summer brings plentiful grasses, flowers, berries, and insects to eat.

Beluga whales surface to breathe and take a look around.

Snow bunting

Only up north!
Thick fur helps keep polar bears warm.

Seals search for small fish from ice floes.

Pintado

Antarctic Circle

The South Pole has many summer visitors, but few animals can survive the harsh winters. The seawater around it freezes in winter and melts in summer, but the ice always remains frozen on Antarctica.

This octopus lives in the cold, deep waters around Antarctica.

Humpback whales put on a jumping display called breaching.

Only down south!
Emperor penguins are warm-blooded, year-round residents.

11

Bear necessities

Polar bears can be found hanging out on the Arctic ice. Like you, the bears enjoy the sun and the water. Unlike you, they hunt for nice plump seals to eat.

BFF-WORTHY?

☐ YES   ☒ NO

No way. These guys may look cute and fluffy, but they're vicious. Give them their space.

This **fur** is clear. The bear looks white because its coat reflects light. Its skin underneath is black, like its nose.

INFO BITES

Name: Polar Bear

Type of animal: Mammal

Home: The Arctic

Size: Males are up to 11 feet long and 1,700 pounds, about the same as a tiny two-seater car. Females are about half as big, the weight of an average motorcycle.

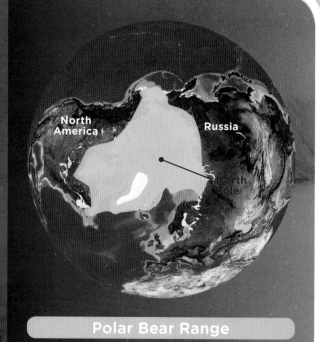

North America   Russia   North Pole

Polar Bear Range

Just like me

Fat under the polar bear's skin keeps it warm—even more than its fur. Your body's fat helps you stay warm, too!

This **nose** knows! A polar bear has a keen sense of smell. It can smell a seal up to 20 miles away.

Paws are big to help the bear swim. Front paws paddle; back paws steer.

13

Food web

Everybody's gotta eat! From tiny plankton, which feed on even smaller plants, to polar bears, which hunt seals, every polar animal is part of the food web.

That's fishy!

The Atlantic puffin catches fish with its beak. When there's a chick in the nest, Mom and Dad take turns bringing fish for it to eat.

Just like me

People eat fish, too. You can catch your own, or find it at a grocery store or restaurant.

Seafood buffet

The rock greenling eats krill, crustaceans, smaller fish, jellies, and algae.

At the top

A polar bear eats seals—their bodies contain lots of fat, which the bear needs to survive.

Big gulp

The humpback whale eats krill and small fish. It filters vast amounts of water to find its prey.

Food and foodie

Tiny plant plankton (phytoplankton) float in the ocean and are eaten by animal plankton (zooplankton).

15

Sky, sea, and land

Some polar animals are landlubbers, while others are at home in the oceans or skies. Some spend time in more than one habitat.

Sea hunt!

Can't hold your breath as long as a seal can? With a snorkel, you can explore the underwater world for a long time.

Critical krill

Countless tons of tiny krill live in all the world's oceans. They eat even smaller plants. Krill are like very small shrimp. They're food for fish, whales, penguins, and other birds.

Long commute

The arctic tern is at home at both poles. It travels from the North Pole to the South Pole and back in search of the longest days and abundant food. It can even sleep while it flies.

Salty snacks

Many animals meet at watering holes, but Dall sheep gather at salt licks. When the snow melts after a hard winter, the sheep lick and eat dirt that's high in salt and minerals.

Take a deep breath

Fur seals can dive down deep in the ocean—up to about 500 feet. They can stay underwater for six or seven minutes before surfacing again.

17

Family face time

Walruses lie on the rocks in heaps that look almost like piles of rocks themselves. They're very sociable and spend time in groups. There's always at least one old guy who spits when he talks, and there is a lot of bellowing. Sound like your family?

Walruses use their **tusks** to pull themselves out of the water.

Just like me
Walruses have five "fingers" on their front flippers.

A **tough hide** protects the walrus from predators—and other walruses!

INFO BITES

Name: Walrus

Type of animal: Mammal

Home: Pacific walruses live along the coasts of Russia and Alaska. Atlantic walruses stay by the coasts of northeastern Canada and Greenland.

Size: 7 to 12 feet long. Males are bigger than females and can weigh up to 3,700 pounds. That's as much as a car.

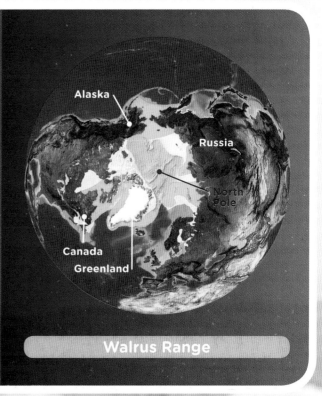

Alaska
Russia
North Pole
Canada
Greenland

Walrus Range

SNUGGLE-WORTHY?

☐ YES ☒ NO

They really want to snuggle only with one another. Plus, they sneeze and snort a lot.

The **flat tail** is small and is normally hidden in a fold of skin.

On the hunt!

There are no supermarkets at the poles. Animals have to work hard for their dinner.

Airborne

Killer whales can catch pretty much anything they want, but penguins have a way to escape. They "porpoise" out of the water, jumping and spinning away.

Wolf pack

Teamwork! Arctic wolves hunt in packs. By working together, they can follow scent trails and take down large animals, such as musk ox and caribou.

Eye spy

A minke whale will sometimes "spy-hop" when hunting for plankton. The whale pokes its head out of the water and scans its surroundings for food.

Seafood, eat food

The Wilson's storm petrel skims the surface of the water looking for tasty bits of plankton to scoop up and eat.

Ice cold

Seals gnaw small breathing holes in the ice and use them all winter long. This ribbon seal is checking things out—no hungry polar bears allowed!

Flipping out

Pinnipeds

Walruses, seals, and sea lions are called pinnipeds. That means "flipper-footed." They spend most of their time in the water, but they also chill out on land and ice.

Harp seal pup

Southern elephant seal

Leopard seal

Northern fur seals

Steller sea lions

Grey seals

Antarctic fur seal

Steller sea lion

Ribbon seal

Pacific walruses

Bearded seals

Weddell seals

Pinniped pals

Some pinnipeds are very social and hang out together. They often hunt in groups, gather in large numbers, and even kiss one another!

Wall-to-walruses

Every summer, about 14,000 male walruses hit the beaches of Round Island in the Bering Sea. Females travel north with their pups.

Hare they are

In winter, the arctic hare looks like a big snowball. You have to look closely to see its ears, nose, and eyes. An arctic hare is one of the few small mammals that can survive in the Arctic cold.

PET-
WORTHY?

☐ YES ☒ NO

Sadly, no. They look so cute and pettable, but they aren't used to people.

The **thick coat** stays white all year round in the coldest parts of the Arctic. In places with seasons, the hare changes to gray in summer, but keeps its cottony white tail.

INFO BITES

Name: Arctic Hare

Type of animal: Mammal

Home: The Arctic tundra and rocky areas

Size: Up to 2 feet long and 12 pounds. It is as long as two small pizzas put together.

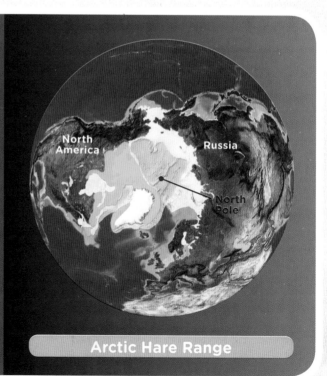

Arctic Hare Range

North America

Russia

North Pole

Short ears keep heat loss to a minimum.

Just like me

When the arctic hare feels threatened, it takes a good look around—then runs!

Strong back legs and **big feet** help the hare escape predators. It is a superfast runner.

Long claws are used to dig for food under ice and snow.

27

Family time

Animals create families of their own, too. Males court the females and when babies are born, parents look after their little ones.

Mom's the word

Beluga whale calves nurse for about two years. Social animals, belugas form large groups called pods. When they grow up, girls stay with their mom, but boys strike out on their own.

I caribou you

Mother and baby caribous are very close. They recognize each other by sight, smell, and sound. If a baby gets separated from its mother during migration, Mom will search until she finds her calf.

Rocking her world

During courtship, a male Adélie penguin will present the female Adélie penguin of his dreams with a single pebble. If she is impressed, they will build a nest of pebbles together. The mother will lay two eggs there.

Twice as nice!

Just like a beluga calf, you can have underwater fun with your mom or dad.

'Tis the seasons

From late March to late September, the sun never sets at the North Pole. The days get shorter and darker as winter arrives. During this time, the South Pole is in complete darkness—then it's daylight for six months.

spring

It's baby time

Warmer weather means nesting time for birds, from snowy owls up north to penguins down south. Both Mom and Dad care for their babies.

When penguins need a new coat, they molt. They lose all their feathers and grow a fresh batch.

summer

Its winter white coat helps the arctic hare hide from a hungry arctic fox.

All dressed up

Many arctic animals wear white all year long. But some change their colors when the snow melts. The arctic hare goes from winter white to summer gray.

all year round

Amazing light shows called auroras appear in the night sky at the poles. Even penguins take on a special glow during these displays.

fall

Eat your veggies

Food can be hard to find in the winter. Plant-eating animals fill up on fresh greens and berries during warm weather, eating as much as they can to fatten up before fall turns to winter.

winter

Ready, set, go!

Polar bear babies are born in winter. They spend their first months in a snow den with Mom, emerging when they're strong enough to make their first journey to the sea ice.

Built to swim

Penguins are birds, but they can't fly. They use their wings to "fly" through the water. They race to catch fish and squid to eat—they spend most of their time in the water.

The **tail** works like a boat rudder for making quick moves.

INFO BITES

Name: King Penguin

Type of animal: Bird

Home: The warmer parts of the Antarctic

Size: Up to 3 feet tall and 35 pounds. That's about the same as a 4-year-old child.

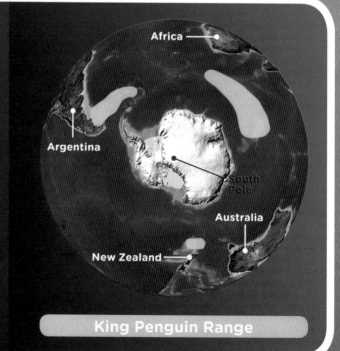

Africa

Argentina

South Pole

Australia

New Zealand

King Penguin Range

Flipperlike wings make a penguin a fast swimmer.

SNUGGLE-WORTHY?

☐ YES   ☒ NO

King penguins are often damp, and they have terrible fish breath. Their stubby little wings would make it hard for them to hug you back.

A **long, thin bill** helps the king penguin grab fish. It swallows the fish as it swims along.

A **light-colored belly** makes the penguin hard to see from below, so predators can't easily find it.

Just like me

The penguin has a clear membrane on its eye, called a third eyelid. It protects the eye in the same way swim goggles protect your eyes.

Unlocking the freezer

Researchers endure harsh conditions to study polar animals. The information they collect tells them what the animals eat, if they are healthy or sick, and if they are moving to new places.

Stay back!

The Ross seal lives on the ice sheets of Antarctica. It eats fish, and so do people. Scientists study the seals' health to be sure that we don't fish so much that too little food is left for them. This one isn't too sure about the researchers!

Catch as catch can

Before scientists can tag an animal, they have to catch it. This elephant seal will have its tag glued on so scientists can keep track of it. By tracking the seal, scientists will be able to measure water temperature wherever it goes.

Tag, you're it!

This walrus is wearing a radio tag that allows researchers to follow it on its journeys. The data tells them when the walrus moves to a new area.

At the rodeo

At a "penguin rodeo," scientists round up penguin chicks for tagging before returning them to their nests. When the penguin corral is empty, the researchers study the poop left behind to see what the penguins have been eating.

35

TALENT: LIVING LARGE

Macaroni penguins live in large colonies, or groups. There can be 2 million or more macaronis in one place. Their name comes from an old phrase that means "very fancy."

TALENT: BOLDNESS

The chinstrap penguin builds its nest out of rocks. There are never quite enough small rocks to go around, so frequent battles over rocks occur among these bold penguins.

TALENT: POSING

The Adélie penguin is noisy and social. It communicates through loud calls, displays, and posturing or posing.

chinstrap penguin

macaroni penguin

adélie penguin

Up to 27 inches tall and 12 pounds

Up to 28 inches tall and 12 pounds

Up to 28 inches tall and 12 pounds

TALENT: SPEEDSTER

The gentoo's little white cap, rounded tummy, and peach-colored feet are adorable. It's also the fastest penguin swimmer, clocking in at 22 miles per hour.

TALENT: LOOKING ROYAL

The king penguin looks a lot like its emperor cousin, only it's number two in size. Like the emperor, it hatches one chick at a time. The little one has fuzzy brown feathers until it's one year old.

TALENT: GREAT DAD

The emperor penguin is famous for its heroic march to breeding grounds and for its long, cold wait for its single egg to hatch. The chick hatches in the harsh winter on its dad's feet.

gentoo penguin

king penguin

emperor penguin

Up to 30 inches tall and 13 pounds

Up to 3 feet tall and 35 pounds

Up to 4 feet tall and 80 pounds

37

Dive-bomb!

Antarctica is the land of penguins. These penguins jump off a diving board made of ice into freezing water. They make the leap in search of a meal.

Baby, it's cold outside

It's supercold at the poles, but polar animals have what it takes to survive. Even the tiniest babies are adapted to the harsh conditions.

Chilly reception

Emperor penguins hatch in the winter, when temperatures can drop to -60 degrees Fahrenheit and the wind blows up to 120 miles per hour. Brrrr!

Out and about

Wolverines dig dens in snowbanks before their babies are born. When the young wolverines, called kits, are old enough to hunt, they move out on their own.

High flyers

Barnacle geese build nests atop 400-foot cliffs to keep their eggs safe. After the goslings hatch, they hurl themselves off the cliffs. They reunite with their parents on the ground and head off together to find food to eat.

Room to grow

Polar bears usually give birth to twins. When the babies are little, the mother and cubs snuggle in their den under the snow. Dens start out as one "room," but the bears add more space over the winter.

Snow for it!

Wonder what it's like to live in a snow den? Build your own next time it snows.

Ice, ice, baby

When you think of the polar world, you probably think of snow, ice, glaciers, and icebergs. Life on—and below—ice is busy at the poles.

Antarctic petrel

Polar bear

Harbor seal

Prowfish

Sea star

Warty bobtail squid

Humpback whale

Sea cucumber

Eelpout fish

Amphipod

White-tailed eagle

Ice floes can be used like flat boats to travel from place to place.

Walrus

Red king crab

Basket star

Glacier
A river of ice that is always moving. Glaciers are formed over years or hundreds of years.

Calving
When a piece of ice falls away from the end of a glacier. Large pieces become icebergs.

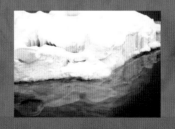

Bergy bit
A medium to large piece of ice that extends 3 to 16 feet above the water.

Growler
Ice pieces about the size of a small truck, with only a few feet showing above the water.

Precious poles

Weather at the poles may seem harsh to humans, but polar animals need the bitter cold and ice to survive. As temperatures at the North and South Poles rise, more and more ice melts, threatening the animals that live there.

Vital ice

Polar bears hunt on pack ice and jump from ice floe to ice floe to get around. As the ice melts earlier and re-freezes later, the bears have a harder time finding food. The bears lose too much weight when summer lasts too long. If polar ice disappears, polar bears could disappear along with it.

Cold is cool

All life in the Antarctic depends on ice. The sea ice contains algae that krill eat. When sea ice melts, there's less algae to feed krill. Fewer krill means less food for fish and penguins to eat.

Comeback kid

Musk oxen predators include wolves, grizzly bears, and humans. They were in danger of extinction until conservation efforts were put in place to save them. Now they live in many places within and around the Arctic Circle.

On the job

Researchers in the Antarctic test the atmosphere for information on climate change.

Vanishing traditions

People who live in the Arctic region rely on the animals there—for food to eat, fur for warm clothing, and bones to turn into tools. Without those animals, their way of life would not be possible.

It's a dog's life

Huskies look like wolves, but they're not. They're dogs. About 4,000 years ago, in Russia, they were bred to work hard. Huskies pulled sleds across the tundra, carrying hunters as they looked for game.

The **eyes** might be blue or brown, or a combination. No matter the color, all huskies have good eyesight.

A **thick, two-layered coat** keeps the husky warm.

Just like me

Siberian huskies look dangerous, but they're not good watchdogs. They're way too friendly.

CUDDLE-WORTHY?

☒ YES ☐ NO

Siberian huskies are great dogs, smart and loving. They make wonderful pets, although they need lots of activity.

INFO BITES

Name: Siberian Husky

Type of animal: Mammal

Home: From Siberia originally but now found all over the world.

Size: About 2 feet high and 35 to 60 pounds. That's about the same as two toddlers side by side.

Siberian Husky Range

Fur grows between the pads of the husky's paws. It helps the dog grip the snow . . . or slide across the kitchen floor.

The old ways

Humans have lived and worked in the Arctic for thousands of years. The Inuit and Inupiat are two groups of native peoples who call the Arctic home. They follow a traditional way of life and use ancient methods to hunt, stay warm, and travel.

Time travel

Everything about this picture—hunter, ice, clothing, weapon, and prey—would have looked about the same 100 years ago. The traditional way lives on.

Man's best friend

For thousands of years, Inuit people have relied on dogs for companionship, hunting, and transportation.

Just like me

Dogs may be at work in your school or community. Service dogs assist people who are blind or need help in other ways.

Hunting at sea

Even though whale hunting is no longer allowed in many countries, the Inupiat have special permission because it is part of their culture. Using a seal-skin boat and old-fashioned harpoons, these Inupiat have captured a bowhead whale. It will feed many families.

Fresh and frozen

Want some fresh fish in the Arctic? Bundle up tight, then drill a hole in the ice and settle down to wait for your dinner to arrive. It could be a long wait.

Can-do attitude

Inuit innovation is boundless. Almost nothing they take from nature is wasted; it is all put to good use. This fishing boat is covered in walrus hide; smaller kayaks have a seal-skin covering.

Reindeer games

Reindeer, sometimes called caribou, are hardy animals and can survive in harsh climates. They're covered in fur from nose to tail to the bottoms of their feet. Reindeer eat greenery in the summer, but in winter they get by on lichen.

INFO BITES

Name: Reindeer

Type of animal: Mammal

Home: The Arctic tundra

Size: Up to 700 pounds, and 5 feet tall without antlers. Antlers can add 3 feet—making them taller than the tallest pro basketball player.

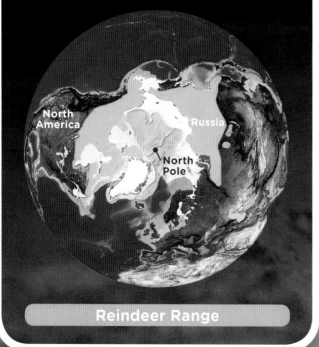

North America

Russia

North Pole

Reindeer Range

Antlers fall off and grow back bigger each year. The branches are called tines—just like the pointed parts of a fork. New antlers are covered in soft fur called velvet.

Just like me

Antlers are like fingerprints. No two sets are the same.

A **woolly undercoat** and top layer of **hollow hairs** trap heat. Air trapped in the hairs warms the reindeer.

STABLE-WORTHY?

☒ YES ☐ NO

Farmers keep domesticated reindeer for the same reasons they keep cows— for milk and meat and muscle. Like cows, these reindeer often seem fond of their owners.

Hairy hooves provide sure footing on ice and snow.

Land of the midnight sun

At the height of summer, in June, the sun shines 24 hours a day in the Arctic Circle. Caribou herds spend their summers on the tundra, feeding on the plentiful grasses and plants found there.

Dressed to impress

Arctic foxes dress for the weather. In summer, they can be seen in formfitting brown or beige suits, tinged with black. For winter, these stylish foxes switch to all-white ensembles that match the snow.

The **ears** can pick up the sound of prey moving around under the snow.

Short legs help the fox hold in body heat. **Paws** have fur between the pads to keep the fox from slipping on ice.

The **fur** is twice as thick in winter as in summer. Underfur adds extra warmth.

INFO BITES

Name: Arctic Fox

Type of animal: Mammal

Home: The Arctic tundra

Size: Up to 2 feet long—about as long as a tricycle. But add another foot for the long tail. Weight is around 10 pounds.

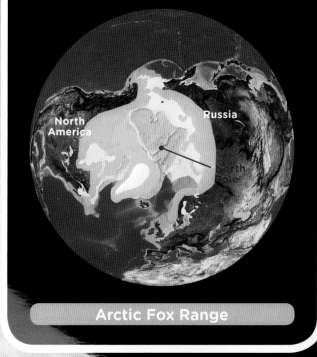

North America

Russia

North Pole

Arctic Fox Range

Just like me

When the wind blows, the arctic fox pulls its fluffy tail over its face like a warm muffler.

Playtime

Yippee! Playtime is fun time. Polar animals have all kinds of playful talents that come in handy in the snow and ice.

Slipping and sliding

You need a sled or a slide, but penguins can just flop down on their tummies and skim over the ice. They love to toboggan!

Rocky road

Polar bears are great climbers. They can scale a ridge or a cliff as easily as you climb on the monkey bars.

King of the hill

Walruses love to hang out. Sometimes they actually sit on top of each other. Still, there can be tussles if a walrus doesn't want to be messed with.

Jumping jacks

Arctic foxes can hear prey moving around under the surface of the snow. Then they JUMP to punch through the snow—and catch a snack.

Ice cold

For a Weddell seal, the world is its fridge. The seal dives deep, then looks up toward the sunlit ice above to spot tasty prey.

Owl be seeing you

Most owls are nocturnal, doing their hunting in the dark of night. But snowy owls are diurnal—they hunt during the day and sleep at night. In the Arctic, summer daylight can last a full 24 hours— plenty of time for getting things done!

Just like me
Baby owls rarely fight, even in a crowded nest. Just like the brothers and sisters you know, right?

Whiter feathers appear on the males as they get older. Females keep some dark marks throughout their lives.

Serrated edges on flight feathers muffle the sound of the owl's wings so it can sneak up on prey.

BFF-
WORTHY?

☐   ☒

YES   NO

A famous young
wizard had one
as a pet. But
razor-sharp
beaks and talons
make these owls
dangerous.

Big eyes help the snowy
owl spot prey.

INFO BITES

Name: Snowy Owl

Type of animal: Bird

Home: The north of Canada, Alaska,
Europe, and Russia. They migrate
farther south in the winter.

Size: Up to 2 feet tall, with a
wingspan of about 4½ feet.
Stretch out your
arms and check
your wingspan—
it's probably
about the same.

North
America

Russia

North
Pole

Europe

Snowy Owl Range

Time to travel

Only a few animals live full-time at the poles. Most migrate, or travel, long distances, following the food and warmer weather.

Long-distance traveler

Arctic terns have the longest migration of all animals. Every year they travel more than 40,000 miles, from their northern breeding grounds to the Antarctic and back.

Keep swimming

Humpback whales make the longest migration of any mammal. In warm weather, they hang out in the Arctic Ocean. They winter near the equator, 5,000 miles away.

Snowy owls

Arctic winters are cold and long. That's when snowy owls, like many people, take off for warm climes and sunny skies.

Moms on the move

As the snow starts to melt in the spring, pregnant reindeer moms migrate to the Arctic coast in search of food. They can walk as many as 1,000 miles. The rest of the herd follow a few weeks later.

Vacation

People often take a trip when it gets cold. But we sometimes head *toward* the cold northern snow.

65

Ice birds

Northern flights

Most Arctic birds head south for the winter to find more plentiful food and warmer weather. In spring, they go north to breed.

Little auk

Tundra swan

Atlantic puffin

Arctic tern

Juvenile skua

Chinstrap penguin

66

Horned grebe

Arctic fulmar

Black guillemot

Gentoo penguin

Giant petrel

Black-browed albatross

Brrr-irds

Penguins galore live in the Antarctic. They share the icy clime with many other birds. Some, like the arctic tern, migrate and live only part-time in the Antarctic.

Seal of approval

Is there anything more adorable than a baby harp seal? A grown harp seal is handsome, too—it's gray, with black marks that form a harp shape. Once the babies are old enough to swim, these seals spend almost all of their time in the water, eating and playing.

The **"tears"** prevent damage from salt. The harp seal always looks like it's been crying.

Just like me
Whether they're swimming (that's most of the time) or sunning, harp seals love to hang out in a group.

The **fluffy white coat** on a baby harp seal lasts for about two weeks. Then the white fur falls out.

Front flippers and **claws** help the seal pull itself over the ice.

INFO BITES

Name: Harp Seal

Type of animal: Mammal

Home: North Atlantic and Arctic Oceans

Size: Up to 6 feet long and 400 pounds. That's the size of two dads.

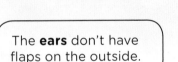

North America

Russia

North Pole

Harp Seal Range

The **ears** don't have flaps on the outside.

COZY-WORTHY?

☐ YES ☒ NO

The babies look so sweet, but Mom and Dad have sharp teeth and strong flippers!

69

Baby faces

Awww... little babies are so cute, and so are little baby animals. Many animal babies stay close to Mom until they are old enough to take care of themselves.

Sibling revelry

Grown-up arctic foxes are white, but babies are brown. Arctic foxes have large litters of five to nine pups, so there's always someone to play with—although not everyone wants to play at the same time.

Nice ice

Baby ringed seals live on the ice while their mothers hunt for food in the water. Mom comes back regularly to check on her pups.

Little hunters

Ermine kits live with Mom in their burrows until they are about eight months old. During this time they learn to hunt, and then they set out on their own.

Mama's moose

Moose babies stay close to Mom for about a year, watching and learning from her, until the next baby is born.

Extreme animals

Polar animals live in extreme conditions. Here are some with special skills and adaptations.

TAKING THE PLUNGE

A polar bear is a strong, steady swimmer. It's a skilled diver, too. A polar bear can dive from the top of an iceberg more than 50 feet into the water. It can also swim long distances—up to 100 miles or more.

HEROIC HUSKY

In 1925, relay teams that included 150 sled dogs raced 674 miles in less than six days through icy blizzards. They were carrying medicine needed to stop a diphtheria

DEVOTED DAD

An emperor penguin father huddles for two months in the cold, dark Antarctic winter, sheltering his one egg. He doesn't eat during this time. Wind chills can dip to -75° Fahrenheit, so the incubating males snuggle together for warmth.

DEEP DIVER

The southern elephant seal can dive more than a mile underwater. That's the deepest dive of any polar marine mammal.

SURF'S UP!

Gentoo penguins can zip through the water in short bursts of up to 22 miles per hour. They don't need a longboard to surf the waves—they use wing power.

HUMONGOUS HEADGEAR

The moose is the biggest animal in the deer family. A male is about 6 feet tall at the shoulder. But what's really impressive are his antlers—they grow up to 6½ feet wide!

epidemic. Balto, a Siberian husky, led the team that made the journey to Nome, Alaska. This feat is celebrated annually by Alaska's famous Iditarod Great Sled Race.

Polar activities

PENGUIN HOP

Imagine you're a penguin and you need to travel across a long stretch of icy cold water, jumping from one ice floe to another.

What you'll need:
- 2 players
- 20 paper plates
- 1 person to be the timer, to call "Go" and determine the winner

1. Make two paths out of paper plates. Use 10 paper plates for each path, and place them a few inches apart on the floor. Decide who will take which path.

2. Line up in front of the first plate in each path. Wait for the timer to call "Go!"

3. Hop from plate to plate and see who can travel fastest from the first ice floe to the last. If you miss an ice floe and fall into the "water," go back to the beginning and start over.

STAR SEAL

What you'll need:
- Drawing paper
- Crayons or markers

Choose a seal from this book and draw a picture of it. Or you can copy this drawing and then color it in. Write down three special things you've learned about the animal from this book.

ARCTIC A-CHORD

What do you think a polar chorus would sound like? Try out the animal sounds below. Invite your friends and family to join together. Have each person choose their favorite animal and mimic its sound and hear what the whole group sounds like.

◀ Polar Bear **rrrroooaaarrrrr**

Seal **arf arf arf arf arf arf arf** ▶

◀ Penguin **cah cah cah cahhhhh**

Walrus **ah-uhr ah-urh ah-urh** ▶

◀ Orca **ah-ee ah-ee ah-ee**

Resources

FIND OUT MORE

Continue your polar adventure and explore more amazing animals by reading more books, checking out interesting websites, and visiting aquariums, museums, and zoos.

PLACES TO VISIT

UNITED STATES

Alaska Zoo
Anchorage, AK
alaskazoo.org
The Alaska Zoo houses a wide variety of polar animals. It is home to musk oxen, polar bears, snowy owls, arctic foxes, Dall sheep, reindeer, harbor seals, arctic wolves, and wolverines. The zoo is active in the conservation of Arctic and sub-Arctic wildlife.

San Diego Zoo
San Diego, CA
zoo.sandiegozoo.org
From the underwater viewing room of the Polar Bear Plunge, visitors can watch playful polar bears in action. The Polar Cam follows their day-to-day activities. Other Arctic animals at the zoo include arctic foxes, arctic wolves, reindeer, and penguins. The Penguin Cam keeps track of their goings-on.

Denver Zoo
Denver, CO
denverzoo.org
Explore the Northern Shores exhibit and see polar bears, seals and sea lions, and arctic foxes in a naturalistic habitat. Visitors can experience underwater viewing at both the polar bear and the sea lion exhibits.

Indianapolis Zoo
Indianapolis, IN
indianapoliszoo.com
A zoo, aquarium, and botanical garden combined, the Indianapolis Zoo re-creates the natural environment of the Arctic, with polar bears; walruses; and gentoo, king, and rockhopper penguins. Go behind the scenes with the Penguin and Pinniped Adventures.

Maryland Zoo in Baltimore
Baltimore, MD
marylandzoo.org
Visit Polar Bear Watch and encounter polar bears, arctic foxes, and snowy owls. Learn about life in the Arctic from the keepers who care for the zoo's polar bears.

Detroit Zoo
Royal Oak, MI
detroitzoo.org
The Arctic Ring of Life is one of North America's largest polar bear exhibits, encompassing over 4 acres of outdoor and indoor features. Arctic foxes and seals also live there. The 70-foot-long Polar Passage is a clear tunnel where visitors can watch swimming and diving bears and seals. At the Penguinarium, see rockhopper, macaroni, king, and gentoo penguins.

Saint Louis Zoo
Saint Louis, MO
stlzoo.org
Four species of penguin, two types of puffin, and other water birds can be found at the Penguin & Puffin Coast exhibit. Sea Lion Sound combines the Sea Lion Basin and a seasonal sea lion show. Visitors walk through an underwater tunnel into the animals' habitat. The zoo is a world leader in saving endangered species and their habitats. Many of the animals there are threatened in the wild.

Columbus Zoo and Aquarium
Powell, OH
columbuszoo.org
At the Polar Frontier exhibit, visitors walk through an underwater viewing area where polar bears swim all around. Four arctic foxes live at the zoo, and the arctic fox habitat provides a look inside a real den. The Battelle Ice Bear Outpost provides information on how to practice conservation at home and join the effort to save the polar bear.

Omaha's Henry Doorly Zoo and Aquarium
Omaha, NE
omahazoo.com
The Durham's Bear Canyon exhibit features polar bears swimming in a 30,000-gallon pool with above- and below-water viewing. Noisy colonies of penguins can be found at the facility's aquarium.

Philadelphia Zoo
Philadelphia, PA
philadelphiazoo.org
Polar bears from the Arctic are among the species that live in the Bear Country exhibit. The Philadelphia Zoo partners with Polar Bears International (PBI) in conducting and promoting research, education, and action-based programs that address the issues endangering polar bears.

CANADA

Calgary Zoo
Calgary, AB
calgaryzoo.com
Surround yourself with playful penguins "walking the waddle." See gentoo, rockhopper, and king penguins perching on rocky outcroppings and plunging into chilly water. Learn about these flightless wonders at behind-the-scenes experiences and Breakfast with the Penguins.

Toronto Zoo
Toronto, ON
torontozoo.com
A state-of-the-art polar bear habitat is at the heart of the 10-Acre Tundra Trek exhibit, which also includes snow geese, arctic foxes and wolves, reindeer, and snowy owls. The zoo has a highly successful breeding program and works closely with conservation institutions, including Polar Bears International (PBI).

BOOKS

ANIMALS: A VISUAL ENCYCLOPEDIA
Meet more than 2,500 amazing animals in this comprehensive, family-fun, global reference guide from Animal Planet—your source for all things animal. Explore the many ways animals are just like us. The book includes more than 1,000 stunning photos!

OCEAN ANIMALS
A companion to POLAR ANIMALS, this Animal Bites book takes the reader on a journey through the oceans. Learn about marine animals from around the world, and see how and where they live.

WEBSITES

You can visit all of the zoos online to learn more. Here are some additional websites to check out.

climatekids.nasa.gov
Learn about the oceans, animals, and Earth's climate, play games, watch videos, and find crafts and activities on this informative and fun kid-friendly website from the National Aeronautics and Space Administration.

coolantarctica.com
Find a comprehensive guide to the southernmost continent, with pictures, facts, quizzes, and information on the animals that live there.

discoverykids.com
Check out polar bears, penguins, and many other animals, play games, and watch videos at this entertaining animal site for kids.

oceanservice.noaa.gov/kids
Start here to find many informative and fun websites from the National Oceanic and Atmospheric Association. Learn about life at the North Pole, follow the South Pole webcam, and find fun activities and photos galore.

Glossary

Antarctic Relating to the South Pole.

Arctic Relating to the North Pole.

Arctic Circle The area around the North Pole.

Arctic region The area north of the tree line, larger than the Arctic Circle. The landscape is frozen, and few plants grow there.

▼ **aurora** Broad bands of light that appear in the night sky, especially in the polar regions. At the North Pole, this is the aurora borealis; at the South Pole, this is called the aurora australis.

An **aurora borealis** is most visible in the dark Arctic winter.

bergy bit A medium to large piece of floating ice that extends up to 16 feet above the water.

breach To leap out of the water. Whales and dolphins breach.

breeding The process of mating and producing babies.

calving When a piece of ice falls away from a glacier. Large pieces of ice become icebergs.

▼ **camouflage** A way of hiding by blending in with the surroundings.

An arctic hare has white fur in winter for **camouflage**.

cold-blooded Having a body temperature not regulated by the body and close to that of the environment. Fish are cold-blooded.

colony A group of animals living in one place. Penguins live in colonies.

conservation The protection of animals, plants, and natural resources.

▼ **courtship** The behavior of animals that leads to mating and breeding.

King penguins embrace during **courtship.**

diurnal Active during the daytime. A diurnal animal sleeps at night.

equator An imaginary line around the middle of the earth. It is hot by the equator.

food web The complex network of food chains in a habitat.

glacier A large mass of ice that moves very slowly across the land.

growler A small piece of floating ice that shows only a few feet above the water.

habitat The place where an animal usually lives, or an area where a variety of animals all live together.

herd A group of animals that live together. Reindeer live in herds.

hibernation The act of sleeping through the winter to conserve energy.

ice floe A sheet of floating ice.

ice sheet A mass of ice that covers land and is bigger than 20,000 square miles. There are two ice sheets on Earth, one in Antarctica and one in Greenland.

incubate To sit on eggs so they will become warm and will hatch.

invertebrate An animal without a spine.

krill A type of zooplankton, like tiny shrimp.

lichen A small plant-like organism that grows on rocks. Many arctic animals eat lichen.

mammal An animal that produces milk to feed its young, has hair on its body, and has a backbone. Humans and polar bears are mammals.

▼ **migration** The movement of animals from one place to another place according to the season.

*Their summer **migration** helps musk oxen find plentiful plants to eat.*

molt To lose hair, feathers, or fur and replace it with new growth. Arctic foxes molt in spring and fall.

nocturnal Active at night. A nocturnal animal sleeps during the daytime.

pack ice Large pieces of floating ice that come together to form a single mass of ice.

pinniped A type of aquatic animal with four flippers as limbs.

plankton Very small plant and animal life in oceans, lakes, and other water. Phytoplankton are tiny plants. Zooplankton are tiny animals.

polar region The area around one of the poles.

predator An animal that hunts and eats other animals.

prey An animal that is eaten by other animals.

school A group of fish.

▼ **spy-hop** To stick the head out of the water to look around. Whales and dolphins spy-hop.

*A humpback whale will **spy-hop** to check out a nearby boat.*

talon The sharp claws on the feet of some birds, especially birds of prey.

tundra Flat land in the Arctic region. No trees can grow there and the deep soil is always frozen.

tusk A long, large tooth that sticks out of an animal such as a walrus.

vertebrate An animal with a spine.

▼ **warm-blooded** Having a relatively high, constant body temperature that is independent of the environment. Birds and mammals are warm-blooded.

*People are **warm-blooded**, but we need to bundle up to stay warm in cold weather.*

Index

Illustrations are indicated by **boldface**. When illustrations fall within a page span, the entire span of pages is **boldface**.